PAUL SIMON

W9-CQS-062

Order No. PS 11345
US International Standard Book Number: 0.8256.3315.X
UK International Standard Book Number: 0.7119.4173.4

Exclusive Distributors:
Music Sales Corporation
257 Park Avenue South, New York, New York 10010 USA
Music Sales Limited
8/9 Frith Street, London W1V 5TZ England
Music Sales Pty. Limited
120 Rothschild Street, Rosebery, Sydney, NSW 2018, Australia

Printed and bound in the United States of America by
Vicks Lithograph and Printing Corporation

THE VERYBEST
a collection of his greatest hits

Contents

The Boy In The Bubble

Words by Paul Simon
Music by Paul Simon and Forere Motloheloa

It was a
It was a
It's a

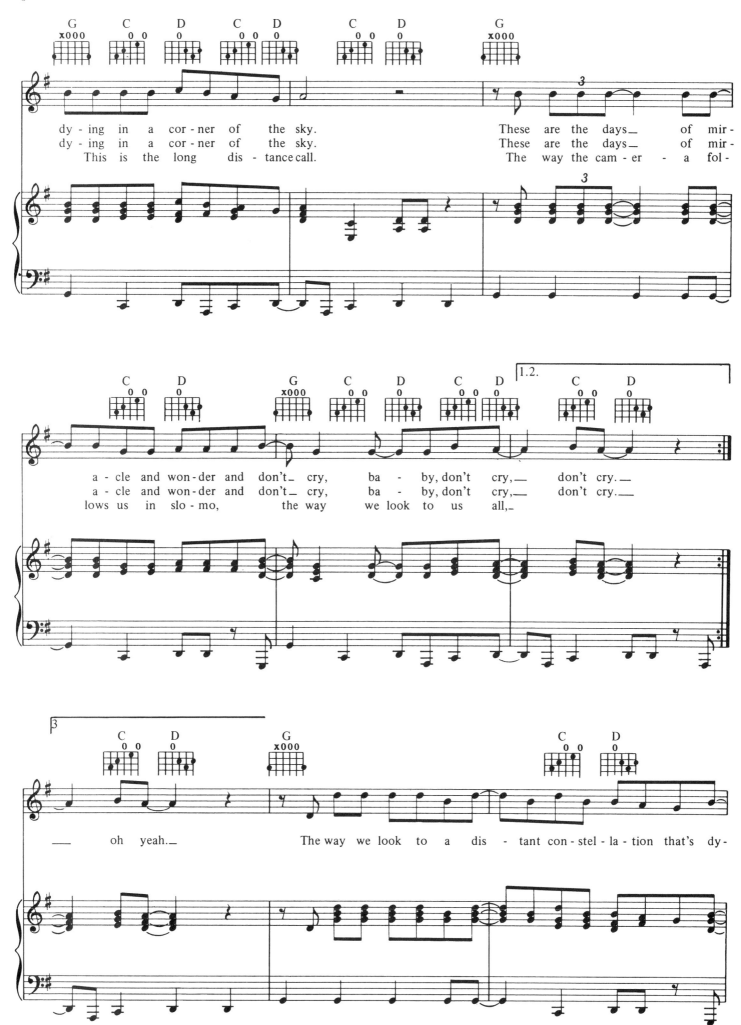

America

Words and Music by Paul Simon

The Boxer

Words and Music by Paul Simon

go - ing home.

In the clear - ing stands a box - er, and a fight - er by his

trade, And he car - ries the re - mind -ers of ev - 'ry glove that

laid him down_ Or cut him till he cried_ out in his an - ger and his shame,_

Bridge Over Troubled Water

Words and Music by Paul Simon

Diamonds On The Soles Of Her Shoes

Words and Music by Paul Simon
Beginning by Paul Simon and Joseph Shabalala

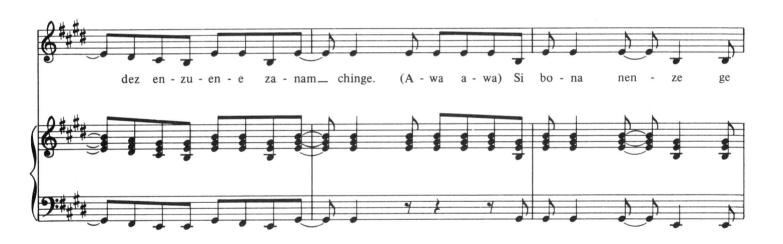

Fifty Ways to Leave Your Lover

Words and Music by Paul Simon

lov - er,   fif - ty ways to leave your lov - er."   Just slip out the
lov - er,   fif - ty ways to leave your lov - er."

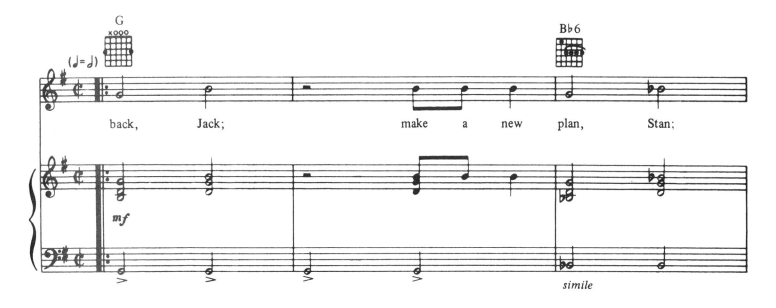

back,   Jack;   make a new plan, Stan;

you don't need to be coy, Roy,   { just get your - self free. }
                       { just lis - ten to me. }

The 59th Street Bridge Song
(Feelin' Groovy)

Words and Music by Paul Simon

Moderately

Slow down,___ you move too fast.___ You got to make the morn-ing last.___ Just kick-in' down the cob-ble stones,___

no deeds to do, no prom-is-es to keep. I'm dap-pled and drow-sy and

read-y to sleep. Let the morn-ing-time drop all its pet-als on me.

Life, I love you, All is groov-y. _____

Repeat and fade out

A Hazy Shade Of Winter

Words and Music by Paul Simon

46

Graceland

Words and Music by Paul Simon

Homeward Bound

Words and Music by Paul Simon

Late In The Evening

Words and Music by Paul Simon

The

first thing I___ re-mem-ber, I___ was ly____ - ing in___ my bed.___
next thing I___ re-mem-ber, I___ am walk - in' down_ the street.___
learned to play__ some lead__ gui - tar._ I was un-der-age__ in this

59

The first thing I___ re-mem - ber when you came___ ___ in - to my life,___ I said, "I'm gon-na get that girl__ no mat-ter what_ I do."

Well, I

D.S. ℅ al Coda ⊕

Coda ⊕

Repeat and fade

I Am A Rock

Words and Music by Paul Simon

Loves Me Like A Rock

Words and Music by Paul Simon

Me And Julio Down By The Schoolyard

Words and Music by Paul Simon

Mother And Child Reunion

Words and Music by Paul Simon

Mrs. Robinson

Words and Music by Paul Simon

We'd like to help_ you learn to help your-self. _____ Look a-round you, all _ you see_ are sym-pa-thet-ic eyes, _____ Stroll a-round _ the grounds_ un-til you feel at home._ And here's to you _

D.S. al Coda

85

The Obvious Child

Words and Music by Paul Simon

Brightly, with a driving beat

1. Well, I'm ac-cus-tomed to a smooth ride, __ Or may-be I'm a
dog who's lost ____ its bite. _____ I don't ex-pect to be treat-
ed like a fool __ no more, ____ I don't ex-pect to sleep __ through the night.

Scarborough Fair/Canticle

Arrangement and original counter melody by Paul Simon and Arthur Garfunkel

Moderately slow

Slip Slidin' Away

Words and Music by Paul Simon

Still Crazy After All These Years

Words and Music by Paul Simon

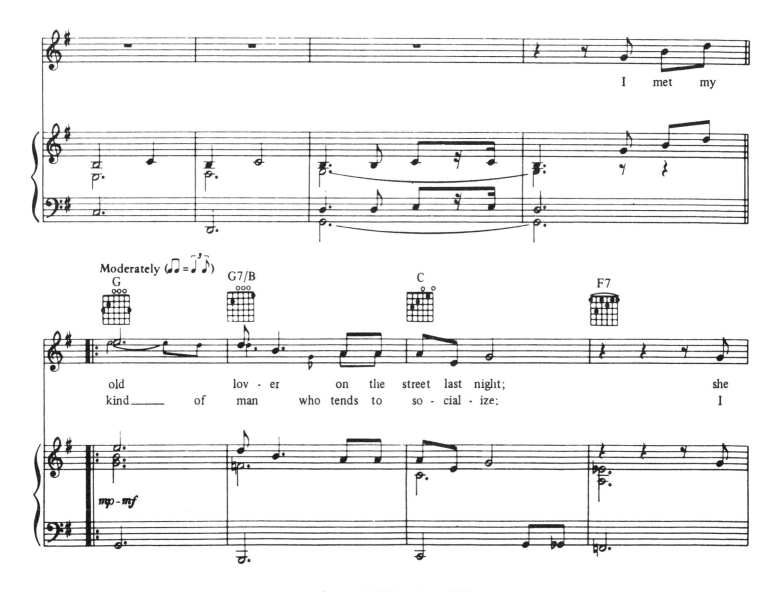

The Sound Of Silence

Words and Music by Paul Simon

You Can Call Me Al

Words and Music by Paul Simon

123

Kodachrome™

Words and Music by Paul Simon

With a moving beat

Verse 1.

1. When I think back ____ on all ____ the crap ____ I learned in high ____

____ school,

It's a won-der